Girl, Bye!
Mindset Makeover
journal for
STEPMOMS
UNFILTERED

DEDICATION

This is for any woman bold enough to try her hand at being a stepmother. I admire you. You've got to be a little nuts, but I admire you nonetheless.

This Book of Badassery Belongs To:

_____

You were born to WIN
You deserve to be happy
A Higher Power is shining on you
Every day you rise is a chance to prosper
No one can steal your joy
You have the power to change your mind
Today is a new day
You can handle this

This journal is all about **you**. Not her. Not him. And not them.

Stepmotherhood is a messy, unpredictable thing, so I wanted to put together a book that mirrors our sentiments. This journal has think pieces, humorous memes, provocative thoughts, and blank pages intentionally strewn about. When I sent my editor the first draft, I reminded her that this is not a formal body of work. I wanted the tone to be conversational and fun. I wanted women to hear my voice as they are going through the pages. If you're looking for cutesy-bubblegum shit, this ain't it. Cutesy-bubblegum shit has never been my testimony, and it's probably not yours either.

As a stepmom in a high conflict situation, the easiest approach is to give in to feelings of detachment, resent, and anxiety. *Girl, Bye!* *Mindset Makeover Journal For Stepmoms: Unfiltered* challenges you to no longer allow your circumstances to dim your light. Sometimes it's a struggle just to be happy because being a stepmom means there are factors beyond your control that affect your entire life. As you navigate your journal, you will learn how to silence the toxic behaviors of others so they no longer take up space in your brain. You will also learn key tactics that will help you gain control over your emotions and find balance after being triggered. *Girl, Bye!* *Mindset Makeover For Stepmoms Unfiltered* is a funny, spicy masterpiece for the Stepmom that wants to get back to enjoying her marriage, her family and her life.

I created this journal to be an emotional tour guide through all of the things that you feel as a stepmom; love, pain, disgrace, fear, and hope. Grab your highlighter and post-it notes. Use your pen frivolously all over the pages! By the time you've read every page, this book should look used and abused! As your sister in the fold, I see you and I've been there. There was a time in my life when this role was responsible for 100% of my anxiety, but literally took up only about 20% of my time. That means even when I wasn't actively *stepmothering*, I still allowed it to seep into the forefront of my psyche and cause me grief. Once I realized that I'd formed a habit of giving over my power to a situation in which I had no positive influence, I began to get a grip on my reality slowly. When your expectations are not aligned with your reality, you will always be in a constant state of chaos.

WHEN YOUR EXPECTATIONS ARE NOT ALIGNED WITH YOUR REALITY, YOU WILL ALWAYS BE IN A CONSTANT STATE OF CHAOS.

Just like you, my introduction into stepmotherhood traumatized me. It even brought some of my own past traumas to the surface. You see, being a stepmom wasn't part of my plan. However, as I got older, I realized that I'd need to make concessions to my firm "no kids rule." As I negotiated, I thought to myself, "If the kids are older and the baby mama is cool, I could make it work." Boy, did God have a laugh at my negotiables?

As a *real-life* Stepfamily Coach, I've personally helped thousands of women just like <u>us</u> through the 3 most common Stepmom sources of contention:

- A high-conflict biological mother
- A partner that cannot set proper boundaries
- A troublesome stepchild

Unequivocally, many women see the key source of their woes as "the mom" or HCBM, as she's referred to on countless internet discussion forums. So much time is spent dehumanizing this woman, and that is what makes her antics so hard to wrap your head around. What if you were able to see her as *just a girl trying to figure it all out the best way she knows how?*

THE RE-HUMANIZATION OF MY HUSBAND'S EX-WIFE

Many years ago, I would not have been able to refer to her as his ex-wife. I'd come up with a slew of belittling names for Janet, my stepkid's mom. I'd weaponized myself with all sorts of intelligent retorts against the onslaught of crazed phone calls, hate-filled emails and online trolling that began the unpleasant experience of being in a relationship with a man that had a failed marriage and a despicable divorce. Like most women that fall in love with a guy with kids, I was bright-eyed and bushy-tailed. I was hopeful that I would one day be welcomed into my new, ready-made family. My introduction in Janet's life came in like a wrecking ball. It was messy and ugly. I now recognize that it felt like a betrayal for both her and me. She had decided to end her marriage and she now had to navigate single motherhood and a slew of other issues that are not my right to share. I was swept off my feet by (and in love with) her ex. Before she had a chance to navigate the sting of divorce and the guilt of breaking up her family, she had to deal with the fact that her ex had moved on and was in a full-blown committed relationship with a bad bitch like me. As most ex-wives, she was not represented as a fairy-princess. My then-boyfriend, unbeknownst to me, still fresh off getting bowled over in family court, told me his own version of pain and betrayal. Of course, I empathized with him. She was the big bad wolf, and he was the helpless doting dad that put up with years of abuse to be near his children. When she and I became entangled in our own messiness, my experiences only validated his version of who she was. My experiences as a stepmom have required the largest portion of empathy, patience, compassion, and restraint that I have ever had to put to use. The kids have been the easy part (I'll get to that later). Dealing with my Husband's ex has been quite the undertaking, though. I'd often wonder why a woman that filed for divorce from a man would want to try to throw salt on my turn at being his Wife.

I'D OFTEN WONDER WHY A WOMAN THAT FILED FOR DIVORCE FROM A MAN WOULD WANT TO TRY TO THROW SALT ON MY TURN AT BEING HIS WIFE.

Why did I not deserve a fair shot at having a solid marriage? I'd ask him countless times if she wanted him back. I wondered if they did all they could to save their marriage. Despite the personal attacks that were aimed at me, I took solace in the inalienable fact that I had no hand in their union coming apart. For some women, becoming a stepmom means that a family has been rocked by the devastation of divorce or separation. For others, their presence seems like a deliberate agitation to an already, unstable coparenting dynamic. No matter how you slice it, many of us have earned our roles as Stepmoms because someone else lost something. Life as they knew it would be forever changed. All of their hopes, dreams, and plans are now skewed by the stain of divorce, separation or single motherhood. Yes, it is a stain. It cannot be washed away, either. Some families find ways to make life better post-breakup. But mine was not so lucky in the beginning.

For years, I watched my Husband schlep 1200 miles to and from family court. Right after our engagement was announced, he had to travel out of state 15 times for court! There were fights over assets, custody, fraudulent accusations, and outright lies being told. It was ugly. And it made coparenting a laughable afterthought. Our family was at war, and our separate households had different stakes in the fight. Through the darkest moments, the children were exposed to some very adult confrontations. I am still utterly repulsed at what I witnessed. My Husband was subjected to years of alienation, which was easy, as he resides in a different state from his children.

In 2016, when I created my first successful online community, I did not intend for it to become a big gathering place for millennials in stepfamilies. One of the most beautiful surprises is that my audience, supporters, and clientele are so diverse. I personally think it's cool that women and men respect my message so much that they support the heck outta me! I certainly had no clue that I'd be coaching others through the murky waters of blending! All I knew is that I was hurting and I needed a space to express myself. At the beginning of my personal journey, I did not want to create a group exclusive to stepmoms because I genuinely wanted to get into the minds of biological mothers and, perhaps, crack the code. While the one in my life was not available to have a transparent conversation with me, I began to befriend 1000s of women online that were more than happy to help me to break down the profanity-laced texts into a more humane form. They happily shared their own drama with me. While I found the conversations extremely comforting, these women found my questions extremely therapeutic.

Understanding the way humans process conflict and grief became so intriguing to me that I put my degree in Family and Consumer Sciences to use. I even got certified as a Family Life Educator. I currently fill my days coaching men, women, children and families, producing content, doing TV and radio stuff, and dealing with all the bells and whistles that come along with my brand. I never represent my life or my family life to be perfect, because it is not. That's just not real. As I help clients navigate their own bouts with anxiety, court battles, and other issues, I, too, am personally evolving. As new studies and best practices are being introduced in the professional journals in which I contribute and subscribe, my methods grow. Life is a constant evolutionary process, and the most progressive humans I know, recognize and relent to change.

LIFE IS A CONSTANT EVOLUTIONARY PROCESS, AND THE MOST PROGRESSIVE HUMANS I KNOW, RECOGNIZE AND RELENT TO CHANGE.

A few summers ago, there were rumblings that my stepkids would possibly be allowed to be with us, in our home, out of their home state for summer visitation! Like many men, my Husband was exhausted when he signed his divorce decree and custody agreement, so the original paperwork was not in his favor. Despite living in a different state, he signed the document that mandated that he was never to take the kids more than 50 miles away from their custodial home without permission from their mom. This gave way to financial abuse, parental alienation, and gross misinterpretations of his paternal rights. Like many of you, we experienced some very bad times because of unhealed emotions. Because of years of disappointments, I did not let myself fall into the trap of hope. Being a stepparent means that you have very little control over things at times. When my Husband purchased 4 roundtrip plane tickets (1 for himself and 3 for the kids), I felt a pang of anxiety. He was not only excited, but he fully believed they would board the plane with him. When he and I got an email of the summer "rules" from the kid's mom, we shook our heads, but I quickly recognized that Janet was attempting to insert a final bit of control because, for the first time in five years, she would not be the gatekeeper between my Husband and his kids. While the list of rules was egregious, disrespectful, and belittling, I realized that this is what it took for her to feel okay. As she instructed, I replied with, "I agree." I wondered why she'd insisted that I do not post photos of her kids or touch their hair, but she neglected to answer my questions about their shoe size, their favorite cereal, or the unique needs of my teen stepchild. By her own design, she had spent many years as the sole caretaker for these children, so I imagine she must have been wrecked with worry. But by trying to prove a point, she robbed herself of having more free time. While she would be eviscerated each time my Husband and I took an international excursion, he had to remind her that she told him he couldn't get the kids on 'that' particular weekend. We chose not to sit home and sulk about the stolen time. Instead of paying a $3000 retainer to file pointless contempt charges, we saved our money and turned the foolish behavior into our FUEL. Everyone may not agree with our approach, but we prayed long and hard, and this is what was best for our family. I remember complaining to one of my single mom friends about the frequently denied visitations. She said, "Girl, enjoy the time with your man because one day she's gonna get tired of keeping up mess. Those kids will be with you two. She'll want to heal, travel and maybe find love. And most of all, she will need a BREAK!"

When my Husband called to tell me he got the kids, and they were all boarding their flight, I was a little shocked. "Hot damn!" I thought! This is really happening. The children arrived with a backpack and their handheld devices, and I'd already shopped for 30-days worth of clothes, shoes, underwear, and anything else I thought they would need for their summer vacation. Here we were, a family of 5 in our too-small Manhattan flat. There was a level of discomfort at the beginning, but my Husband is amazing at making everyone feel at ease. After a few days, we all settled into just being a family. Something else also began to happen.

As I watched these well-adjusted, well-mannered children, thoughts of their mother crept in. How could this *thorn in my side* raise such balanced kids?! They seemed to love and admire her. She expressed love for them. How could a woman raise so much hell, but also raise such decent little humans? For the first time ever, the thought crossed my mind that I was only seeing her from a singular perspective. She had been a deliberate source of pain in my life, BUT she also could only see me as a painful reminder that her own circumstance had permanently shifted. She was not afforded a moment to take a beat and get herself and her kids acclimated to the fact that daddy had a new boo. This woman was still hurting and hurt people really do try to hurt people. If I could learn to view her from the eyes of her children, I could possibly extend compassion to her in a way that would allow forgiveness and healing on my own part.

IF I COULD LEARN TO VIEW HER FROM THE EYES OF HER CHILDREN, I COULD POSSIBLY EXTEND COMPASSION TO HER IN A WAY THAT WOULD ALLOW HEALING ON MY OWN PART.

You see, it is easy to encompass a deliberate detachment from a pure stranger. However, when you get down to the root of a person's humanity, you understand them. You may even feel sorry for them. In turn, you also learn to protect yourself from their antics. They cannot control themselves or their own emotions. Imagine how much of a living hell it must be to wreak havoc in someone's life intentionally?! Pat yourself on the back friend; at least you're not them....

As all good times, summer break came to an end and the kids and I made a scrapbook of all of our fun summer memories. The four of us sat sprawled on the floor and filled our different books with photos I'd printed, and we reminisced on our fun times. My stepson noticed that I had removed all of the photos of me from his stack. He asked me why he could not have any photos of me. I did not want to tell him my REAL reasons, and before I knew it, he came and grabbed a few of his favorite photos of us at the beach. I quietly asked the eldest child if she thought it would create drama if there was a photo of me and she simply said, "Maybe just one." Moments later, I saw my 13-year old stepdaughter leave the room with one of the scrapbooks. My Husband sent me a text; it said, "She texted her mom and told her they were bringing a scrapbook home. She told them not to bring any pictures of you into her house." That moment hit me hard. I expected that Janet was devoid of compassion on anything remotely related to me, but I was taken aback that it had been festering under my own roof. I had to excuse myself, and I wept. I lamented to my Husband that I'd spend $200 getting photos printed and on scrapbooking materials. The fact that this young girl seemed to contribute to the chaos hurt like hell. Why would she do this, I thought? Ultimately, I realized that my stepdaughter, being the oldest, not only served as the liaison, but she might have feared the responsibility of coaxing feelings of discomfort when her mom viewed the laughs, love, and great time that was evident in those scrapbook photos. It was a self-preservation move, and I can't blame her. Ultimately, I called my stepdaughter to our bedroom, and I told her how I felt. She saw my 'ugly cry.' I explained that I loved her and I appreciated the bond we built during the summer. I told her that I understand why she did what she did. I apologized that she was caught in the middle of "all the adult bullshit." I also told her that one day, she would be able to decide for herself where she'll place me in her life. Our relationship does not automatically include the unconditional love she, her mom and dad have for one another. She and I have to choose one another and actually put in work to fortify something real. I asked her to please chose me one day. She said ok. My stepdaughter, her father and I shed a few tears. We all felt the finality and dismantling of the oneness that we had forged during the summer. It seemed like the closer the kids got to their departure for the airport, the more separation anxiety began to set in. Everyone in the house was sad and quiet on the last day. As a true Queen does, I dusted myself off, and I sent the kids home with their individual scrapbooks and framed photos to give their mom.

A few days later, *someone* sent me a text (from a new number) and said, "Hey ugly. Why would you buy a 6-year old a bra? You can't be this stupid."

First of all, me, ugly?

Show me where?!

I'll wait... I'm still waiting.

And for clarification, I bought my stepdaughter undershirts and underpants. Because it's 90 degrees in the summer, some of the undershirts were cropped. They were always worn underneath a full-length t-shirt or dress.) Per usual, I screenshotted the message and put it in File 13, my garbage heap file. Sidenote: I swear one day, I'm gonna compile all of these crazy-ass texts and emails into a funny coffee table book. Anyone that cannot speak to me respectfully finds themselves a permanent home in my BLOCK folder.

I'm able to bounce back SO fast after these negative interactions because I have completely rehumanized this woman. One must be committed to QUIT seeing their stepkid's mother as a worthy adversary. She is not a big, bad monster. Perhaps she has attempted to steal, kill and destroy your household, but each time, you have prevailed, haven't you?! The day you realize

13

that you are merely a soldier in a war that a woman is fighting within herself is the day you will exit the battlefield.

THE DAY I REALIZED THAT I WAS MERELY A SOLDIER IN A WAR THAT A WOMAN WAS FIGHTING WITHIN HERSELF, I LEFT THE BATTLEFIELD.

I refuse to give in and fight with any human that is entranced by trauma and who willingly resides in chaos.

That's like letting a toddler drive my car so their tantrum will stop.

TASK: We all know that toddlers will wig out for the zaniest reasons. My godson once had a full-blown meltdown because I told him he couldn't grow a tail and become a baby dragon. I want you to envision yourself in the midst of a kid in full tantrum mode because you won't let them drive your car. Now imagine YOURSELF giving your car keys to this toddler. They crank the car up, put it in gear and drive it off a cliff.

FORM THE HABIT of inserting this mental picture in your mind EACH time, you find yourself sucked into a conflict with someone. Your keys represent your **peace of mind**. When you hand over the keys to a human that is incapable of taking you to a positive place, you've lost control, and a disaster happens.

All likenesses and similarities in this story are strictly coincidental. Certain facts have been changed to support the narrative of this piece.

What's your story?

Fixed Mindset

- Avoids challenges
- Gives up easily
- Sees effort as pointless
- Ignores helpful negative feedback
- Feels threatened by gains of others
- Takes rejection as a sign of defeat
- Prioritizes the needs of others to a fault
- Unable to set personal boundaries

Growth Mindset

- Embraces challenges
- Persists in the face of setbacks
- Sees efforts as a path to mastery
- Learns from criticism
- Feels lessons and inspiration in success of others
- Sees rejection as an opportunity to grow or reroute
- Self care is paramount
- Respects boundaries and sets firm boundaries

if she doesn't like

HERSELF

she can't possibly like YOU

One of my favorite topics to tackle is the HCBM, the She Devil, the Thorn in your side! So many Stepmoms live in a constant state of anxiety because their man's coparent is the ferocious embodiment of their worst nightmares.

Honey, she's NOT the big bad wolf. She is NOT some mythical swamp creature that you should revere. She is just looking for a place to transfer her bad energy.

She's just a girl that has not learned how to sort out her feelings. She is insecure. She is deathly afraid of YOU. To HER, you're the MONSTER from her nightmares… one that her kids' dad is in love with and one that her kids might fall for too.

Do you NOT see how POWERFUL you really are? If a woman would try her damnedest to destroy your man, his happiness, and her kid's emotional well-being, this isn't about YOU. In fact, your hurt feelings are just the collateral damage to her mission of destruction. That does not make it hurt any less, but hopefully you have a bit of perspective, so you will form the habit of not taking these annoyances personally. It's not your job to disarm her attacks. You just need to take cover in "the lane" you've been told to stay in.

When a person is led by fear, they either retreat or attack. The Mama Bear that you have the opportunity to coexist with has convinced herself that she must avenge her territory. As she spends her energy on being terrible, your mission is to understand her behaviors and use your knowledge to become an impenetrable hater-blocker.
By the time you've completed your journal, your mind will be a fertile ground to:

- ❖ receive love
- ❖ delightfully detach from bullshit
- ❖ discard bullshit
- ❖ build a boundary wall so bullshit can't get through
- ❖ silence hateful texts, emails and words (and bullshit)
- ❖ be the most #TeamUnbothered gal in the land (no bullshit)

Just for shits and giggles, I've put together a list of the common baby mama-isms. You're not alone, I swear. Here's a list of some lovely sentiments you have probably heard or that will be most certainly thrown your way:

- ✓ **He wants his family back** (Bitch, he wants his kids. Stop hatin'. He'd rather have a football-sized hemorrhoid than you. He'd rather eat a jalapeno and laxative pizza.)
- ✓ **My kids hate you** (Nah, you're just afraid that they'll love me as much as their dad does. Don't worry. They will.)
- ✓ **You're a downgrade** (insert crying laugh emoji)
- ✓ **He's changed since he got with you** (Isn't that the point. Listen, I have nothing to do with the experience you had with him. And people can change, but at his core, he's still the same good man you fell for. You know he's a great dad. Whatever your experience was, trust that he is implementing all the lessons he learned with you. So thanks, I guess. As a token of my appreciation. I will take great care of him and my stepkids. Sounds like a win for everyone.)
- ✓ **What kind of woman would be with a deadbeat like him?** (Oh, brother. What kind of woman would have babies by him then fight him tooth and nail to keep those babies away?)
- ✓ **I'm the love of his life. He'll never love you like he loved me** (You *were* the love of his life and thank heavens for growth. Try it.)
- ✓ **I sucked up all his good years, enjoy my sloppy seconds** (I'm sorry. I quit listening after "I sucked.")
- ✓ **My kids don't see you as a stepmom, you're just their dad's wife** (That's fine, but every time they're around me, they will have the privilege of observing their father being loved and cherished.)
- ✓ **You'll never be close to my kids** (Have you noticed that each time you speak death towards me, you're actually giving me life? Keep it comin' boo.)
- ✓ **You're ugly/fat/stupid** (And you're a supermodel/thin/genius? Do you live in a funhouse?)
- ✓ **I hate him! I don't want him!** (Sounds like you're trying to convince yourself of that because everyone else can see right through you.)
- ✓ **My kids hate it at your house** (They hate that you won't release them from this invisible vendetta that you're fighting within yourself. Either way, I'm as happy as a clam at MY house.)
- ✓ **You ruined my family** (Girl, Bye! that was all your handiwork.)

but did you die?

DOES SHE RUN YOUR HOUSE?

Do your kids hate you?

IF SHE EVAPORATED, WOULD YOU?

DOES SHE PAY YOUR BILLS?

can you breathe?

are the sun and moon still in the sky?

Does your man love you?

is life worth living?

ARE YOU STILL A BAD BITCH?

DOES A BEAR SHIT IN THE WOODS?

if yes then

reward yourself with a snack and a nap

also 🖕 her

Being a Stepmom is the hardest role I've ever had...

BUT IT'S NOT HARDER THAN...

CoMama Drama

The Breakdown

I've built a really successful coaching practice around Comama Drama. When I began my studies, the question I aimed to answer was, "Why are Mothers and Stepmothers natural enemies?" Much of my focus has shifted to understanding high conflict mothers and teaching stepmothers how to be happy and #TeamUnbothered despite the *hcbm* in their lives.

Essentially, it is intrinsic for this duo to experience contention as they lay claim to their respective territories and express personal expectations. Some women in co-mothering situations find their way toward amicable relationships with a foundation of boundaries and respect while the majority learn to simply tolerate one another.

Over the years, I've found that the root of the Comama conflict is based on four key factors:

1. **Fear**- A mother may feel threatened when a woman treads into a space that she feels should be exclusively hers. She cannot fathom another woman bonding with her child as she does. Her ego, if not checked, will crush a budding stepmom/stepchild relationship because she is afraid she will lose her child's affections. A smart mom knows that her role is irreplaceable; however, even the soundest mothers can feel the pangs of jealousy. Consequently, if she makes efforts to drive a wedge between her child's relationship with their stepmother, she is also usurping her child's ability to develop love relationships based on their own instincts.

   The stepmother's key priority should be to stand as her partner's support as he parents his child. Usually, this takes a backseat due her own emotional trials, conflict, uncertainty of her role and unclear boundaries. Insecurity, especially for a new stepmom is normal; however, if she does not have excellent resources in place to help her cope, then her stepmothering journey will end up being her key stressor.

UNWILLINGNESS TO ACCEPT A NEW ROLE

2. **Unwillingness to accept a new role** - Being in a blended family means one must be flexible and compassionate. When a mother is accustomed to being the leading lady in a man's life, the transition from romantic interest to coparent can be difficult. When her child's father gets a new partner, feelings of resent and confusion can get exacerbated. The mother may not be able to act in the child's best interest because of heartache. However, once a mother can acknowledge that a transition has happened in her life, she can begin to redefine motherhood, coparenting, and even accept that her child will have a new woman to show them what romantic love for their father looks like.

A stepmother must also define her role based on the tools she has been given within her ready-made family. An early assessment of her situation will help a stepmother avoid exhaustive efforts toward circumstances that do not and will never exist for her family.

INABILITY TO ALIGN THEIR EXPECTATIONS WITH REALITY

3. **Inability to align expectations with reality** - Let's say your friend buys a small, fluffy dog, and each time you reach to pet the animal, it growls and bites you. The pattern should show you that no matter how adorable this dog appears to be, it wants to bite your fingers. While most people would expect a pint-sized animal to be lovable, the reality is this particular one is vicious, at least towards you. If you continue to extend your hand, it will get bitten. Unless you are a glutton for pain, aligning the trend of someone's behavior with your expectation of how they will treat you will save your fingers and your peace of mind.

THE MAN IN THE MIDDLE

4. **The man in the middle** - As with all conflicted step-wife combos, these women have vastly different interpretations of the man in the middle. His ex sees him as a villain, and his new wife sees him as a victim turned hero. Their experiences with him are what now bond their future and their family, but their personal perceptions also set the tone for how they approach one another. The new wife sees the ex as an insane, lazy woman. And the ex sees the new woman as the nail in the coffin to her marriage. They are unable to ACCEPT their intersecting circumstances. They have been reluctantly thrown together, but neither woman truly sees the other as a part of her life. They are merely outsiders that will, at most, be tolerated.

    The man in the middle plays a huge role in how the women in his life get along. Most men have no clue how to go about introducing their ex-wife to their girlfriend, so they beat around the bush and cause more harm than necessary. In general, men fear two things in this scenario: They do not want an ex to taint a fresh relationship, or they do not want the two women to get together and compare notes!

    There's a certain finesse that comes along with ensuring that an ex-wife and a new wife are both actively engaged and fully understand their roles. The man in the middle is not responsible for helping an ex to mend her broken heart or handle her personal issues. He should be firm and intentional with his motives as a coparent without divulging his personal business and harming his new relationship. He should also steer clear of making his new woman his dumping ground for the frustrations he has with his ex. This lays the foundation for animosity.

    Most men fail (miserably) while trying to keep both women appeased. This often results in one woman feeling slighted and probably with a bruised ego. Either way, the man in the middle will have hell to pay.

    *The entire **Man in the Middle** portion is an excerpt from my workbook **Girl, Bye! She's Not Going Anywhere...Neither Are You.***

i take

all of the risks

and

responsibilities

but i get none

of the rewards

I wish

MY MAN

WOULD

Personal Reflections

GOD MAKE
ME A BIRD
SO I CAN
FLY FAR
away...

also me as a bird...

try me bitch

I'll shit right in your goddamn mouth

5 things I'd like my stepkids to know about me

5 things I'd like my stepkids mum to know about me

there's a chance they may

NEVER

get to know you for who you REALLY are...

AND YOU'RE GONNA HAVE TO

be okay with that

They may take every beautiful thing about you and turn it into something nasty...

per·spec·tive
/pər'spektiv/
a particular attitude toward or way of regarding something; a point of view.

it means that they're unable to see you from a positive perspective

REFLECTIONS

If you had a chance
to do it all over
again, would you
still say YES?

when surveyed,
72% of Stepmoms
said NO!

No one is holding you hostage, so WHY haven't you thrown in the towel?

CONSTANTLY
REMINDING YOUR
MAN OF HOW
HIS BAD CHOICES
HAVE MADE YOUR
LIFE A LIVING
HELL IS RUDE AND
DISRESPECTFUL

no one's bustin' your chops for your past mistakes

YOURS JUST HAPPENED TO STAY IN THE PAST...

IF I STOP REMINDING MY MAN OF
HOW MISERABLE STEPMOMMING
MAKES ME, I FEAR...

I CAN'T FIX WHAT I

didn't break

LETTING GO DOESN'T MEAN THAT YOU DON'T CARE ABOUT SOMEONE ANYMORE. IT'S JUST REALIZING THAT THE ONLY PERSON YOU REALLY HAVE CONTROL OVER IS YOURSELF.

-DEBORAH REBER

Life is a series of natural and spontaneous changes. Don't resist them; that only creates sorrow. Let reality be reality. Let things flow naturally forward in whatever way they like.

-Lao Tzu

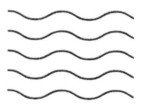

I feel seen when...

To be fully seen by somebody, then, and be loved anyhow - this is a human offering that can border on miraculous.

Elizabeth Gilbert

Queen, choose to take your power back.

If there are circumstances and people that you have allowed to drain your life force and destroy your peace, begin the process of release so you can be restored.

You know what you need to do for your life.

Just make the necessary changes so you can finally be free. Peace is not just the absence of drama.

Peace means wholeness, abundance, nothing lacking.

Peace is your Divine birthright. It is not an option for your life; it should be the standard. Just know this: if you want to reclaim your peace, you must be willing to release.

- Molesey Crawford

Personal Reflections

my triggers are...

how has your partner been traumatized by his coparenting conflict?

A LOT OF STEPCHILDREN ARE GOOD ABOUT HIDING
THEIR EMOTIONAL WOUNDS

My Thoughts

When you finally
learn that
a person's behavior has
more to do
with their own
internal struggle
than it ever did with
you.-
You learn grace.

My definition **of grace is...**

When you find your mind wandering to unhealthy places, come up with a "stop word."
Stop words help us to call out our negative thought patterns and redirect to the present moment.

examples of Stop Words

Girl, Bye!

(insert your name) Wake up!

bitch, you're being dumb again

Sis!   **Back to present**

Nope   **Heal!**

YOU'RE LYING TO YOURSELF AGAIN

NAMASTE

Call out to a Higher Power

MINDSET SHIFT

I REALLY LOVE MYSELF BECAUSE...

ALSO

They tried to bury us.
They did not know we
were seeds.

- Mexican Proverb

I've had many stones thrown at me, and I've survived. I am more than a conqueror. This too shall pass. They may never get better so I will have to get better.

MOMMY & DADDY SITTING IN THE TREE

K-I-S-S-I-N-G

1ST

comes love

THEN THEY BREAKUP

NOW STEPMOM

is pushing the baby

CARRIAGE

Reflections

THINGS I'LL THROW IN MY FUCKIT BUCKET...

Metaphorically, the place you put things that you don't really care about or want to deal with at the time. Also, something you would normally care about, but don't at the moment.

Reflections

When things become overwhelming, you have the right to take off your stepmom hat, hop on your broomstick and fly away!

hi, are you coming back?

IT'S TOTALLY NATURAL TO FEEL OVERWHELMED.

I GIVE MYSELF PERMISSION TO TAKE SOME TIME AWAY WHEN...

It's rare that a HCBM
will have a change
of heart and become
your ally
but
miracles can
happen

A woman that has found solace in centering her life around contention and conflict will be unable to forge a fruitful relationship with you. UNTIL she develops the strong desire to get along and create peace, don't count on her being your ally.

MANIC EPISODES

When you get a barrage of texts or emails, seemingly out of nowhere, take a beat. Do not respond. Consider that the other party may be temporarily triggered and does not have the ability to self-calibrate her emotions.

naja says

Some people are unable to self-calibrate their feelings; therefore, they may lash out when triggered. You can train these people that YOU are NOT a supplier, and they will eventually go elsewhere. BUT, if you answer each time they call, you are showing them that you are a willing participant in their chaos.

Stepmom Mantra

Being a stepmom will not ruin my day

Naja Hall on self-care

Personal Reflections

You may not have been his
FIRST WIFE
but you're his
FOREVER WIFE

Naja Hall on remarriage

Beating yourself (and him) up over a first does absolutely nothing for your happiness. Comparison is the thief of progress, and quite frankly, when you constantly compare yourself to something that's dead, you're the only one that's giving it life. Resurrecting an experience (or mistake) is bad for morale, so should you find yourself rehashing his past, use your "stop word!" If you don't have one, listen to my podcast on Stepmom Affirmations!

Search: I Know I'm CRAZY with Naja Hall: Episode 004 on all podcast apps

I am grateful to be in this position because...

> # will my stepchild ever love me if her mother doesn't like me?
>
> # Sorry, but if your stepchild's mother discourages the child from bonding with you, at best, the relationship will be surface and superficial.
>
> Naja Hall on the ugly truth

(Generally speaking) It is virtually impossible for a stepmother to form a close love bond with a stepchild if their biological mother discourages it. The child will experience feelings of guilt for liking the stepmother. The child will grow to resent nice gestures from her because they will be deemed disingenuous. The child will learn to manipulate because they are being parented by an emotionally manipulative mother. At best, should the child possess a great level of mental tenacity, they will develop a respectful, yet detached relationship with their stepmother.

This makes me feel

It's NOT ok to block a loving father from being able to call his child's cell phone.

Naja Hall on passive parental alienation

If you've felt the pangs of alienation, then you understand how it can attack the fiber of a relationship. One of the key ways of destroying a father/child relationship is to limit communication. This way, the alienating parent can control the narrative and inflict their mission of dividing and conquering. Sometimes covert alienation can occur. A simple word or display of affection can trap a child in a loyalty bind. How has alienation affected your family?

NOTES

 **in her head...**

When I noticed my son was developing a connection with his stepmom, I blocked it. Although irrational, I fear he will think she is better than me.

Naja Hall on Mom's Perspective

our egos are simply our speaking egos louder than louder our conscience. conscience.

Reverse Stepmom Enmeshment

When a stepmom is unable to compartmentalize her feelings of contempt for her stepkid's mom and separate it from her stepkids

We all know about moms that have unhealthy attachments to their children. BUT if you're a stepmom whose stepchild has a high conflict biological mother, sometimes you may have difficulty separating the child from their mother's antics. It's tough NOT to think that a child that is used as their mother's emotional repository will not mirror her behavior. Be mindful that not all children will adopt a temperament of conflict. Some crave love and vulnerability from you. Don't allow the invisible tension to hinder your chance to show love to a child that is yearning for it.

naja says

Not all kids with a HCBM take on her temperament. Be careful not to isolate a stepchild that actually desires a relationship with you.

Feelings of isolation can make a stepmom want to retreat to a safe space. It's natural to want to protect oneself from further pain. But be mindful of shunning a child that demonstrates that they need your affection and tenderness. No matter what, they still need love, and YOU just may be the one to help them release it.

I will give love away. I have an endless supply.

How did your childhood experience with your own stepmom affect how you interact with your stepchildren?

Naja Hall on personal reflection

When I was a child

family photos

It's our baby's 1st Christmas and I set up a photo shoot for our Holiday cards.
I'm thinking of canceling because my stepkids can't come.

I'd encourage this family photo. I wouldn't want my bios missing out on opportunities/memories because their half-siblings couldn't be there. I'm not about martyring myself or my littles because of the unchecked emotions of people that are not under my primary influence.

I'd certainly make every effort to include them sometimes, but I refuse to be stepmom shamed.

I feel Stepmom shamed when

what she said

You may as well have kids with her because you won't see my kids again

what she meant

I know you're a good dad but it hurts to think about you raising the family **WE** planned with another woman. I am angry and I've not learned how to express these feelings in a way that promotes positive coparenting

NAJA HALL TRANSLATES HCBM LINGO

People often let anger and pain cover their ability to be vulnerable. Listen to what she's not saying to get to the root of the issue. Respond to the vulnerable person on the inside as opposed to the conflicted person that is lashing out.

Thoughts

what she said

I'm going to find my kids a new dad

what she meant

Our household has broken up and my dreams of a happy family are crushed. I know I will never have that with you, but I still want our kids to know what a "traditional" home feels like. By bringing another man into our home I think the kids will have some semblance of normalcy.

NAJA HALL TRANSLATES HCBM LINGO

It's common to want to replace that which has been lost. It's wrong to attempt to discard a loving dad because he is no longer a part of the household. Accept that you cannot change her outlook. Write down a few affirmations that will help you change your outlook.

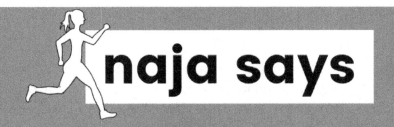

If he's not the BEST man you've EVER been with RUN

Here's your monthly reminder!!! Being a Stepmom comes with a LOT of sacrifices. If he's not worth it, pack your bags and RUN FOREST RUN!!!!

Hmmm...

what she said

I'd rather communicate with you
(stepmom) than my child's father.

what she meant

I have not resolved my bad feelings for BD.
I am not accustomed to him setting
boundaries so I'll use your desire to be a
helping hand against him. I also want to
know what he sees in you that he could
not see in me. Ultimately, I'll turn on you.

NAJA HALL TRANSLATES HCBM LINGO

Don't fall for it. A new well-meaning stepmom will gladly jump at the opportunity to help her man and his child's mother find peace. This is a naive newbie mistake. If the coparenting situation is high conflict, it's best practice to stay in the background and support your man. You didn't make this mess. You don't have to clean it up. Occupy your time with something more productive.

what she said

Why don't you just sign your parental rights away. You don't want my child anyway

what she meant

I do not know how to seperate the relationship you have with our child from the romantic relationship you had with me. It would be easier for me to cope with my singleness if you were gone.

NAJA HALL TRANSLATES HCBM LINGO

This is pretty common when a mother is trying to reconcile her feelings and come to grips with the fact that the life she's planned will be different.

She is hurt, isolated, lost and angry. She knows he's a good dad, but she is so enmeshed with the child that she does not know how to separate her dead relationship with him from a very much alive father/child relationship.

If she doesn't seek help, she'll continue this campaign to alienate him. She may take drastic measures.

Tell your man to ignore the outbursts, disrespect, and harsh language.
Eventually, she will learn that he is not a person that will fuel her angry tirades, and she'll seek another target.

In the meantime, he should focus on NOT having phone conversations with her and limiting contact to email. The only conversation he should entertain is about their child. If money is a point of contention, have him put himself on court-mandated child support and when the mother mentions money, refer her to the orders. The less they communicate about, the less the chances for conflict.

Children usually sympathize with their weaker or more manipulative parent

Coparenting isn't a competition, but it seems that some people are committed to making it so! If your child is aware of how much you don't like their other parent or step-parent, it's because you are secretly afraid of how much they DO like their other parent or step-parent. Your fragile ego cannot accept the fact that you are unable to control who your child loves, so you try to damage how they view the person. It's NOT FAIR that you're teaching your child to see their other parent through the eyes of YOUR unhealed pain. We often weaponize our children because we think that we are doing damage to their other parent. When in fact, the damage that we are inflicting (by including our children in adult bullshit) is devastating to your child's emotional wellbeing. There exists a breed of parent that secretly enjoys when their child rejects the people in their other household. It's sad but true. This parent will alienate in an effort to "get the kid on their side." The child probably loves the people in their other household, but children will actually mirror the behavior of the weaker parent because they know that these people are fragile. A weak parent is one that emotionally manipulates their child by infusing them in adult conflict.

Reflections

Whenever you find a man, I hope his babymama gives you half the hell you've given me.

Don't act like you've never wished upon a star that HCBM will find a man who has a hellion of a BM so that she can see how she's made you feel. Don't be petty; wish her peace and blessings.

Rant

Forbidding your child from NOT liking me isn't hurting me. It's hurting them.

If your stepkids love you, it's because you treat them well. When they are discouraged from showing love back, that takes away their ability to trust their own instincts when building love bonds.

I feel...

Dad's can have Torn Loyalties too

When your man is under the spell of a narcissistic coparent, it will be impossible for him to be present for you.

You're fighting a losing battle if your man still maintains unhealthy ties with his kid's mother. The best bet is to step back, allow them to sort out their "affairs." Trust me, you don't stand a chance when there's a baby mama and a baby daddy that can't let one another go.

Thoughts

Stepdads vs Stepmoms

I'm the only Stepmom my stepkids have ever known but I'm not allowed to be close to them. But they've had 6 "stepdads" and they were encouraged to love them all.

-Alex B.

Sometimes you are going to get the short end of the stick. If a woman is deadset on making sure you are not a key influence in "her" kids' lives, your hands are tied. Take those hands and wave 'em in the air.

Wave 'em like you just don't care! **#TeamUnbothered**

an unbothered stepmom
understands that her key
priorities are herself, her
household and things
within her direct realm of
control

WHAT IS NOT YOUR PRIORITY?

being a stepmom can unearth your own childhood traumas

@VIPStepmom

Watching your stepkids be traumatized by their parents can bring up old traumas for you. Your stepkids can suffer from abandonment issues. They can get caught up in coparenting chaos. They're being shuffled back and forth from house to house. They are stuck in the middle of their parents' drama. This can be RE-TRAUMATIZING for you! Be mindful of how involved you get and make sure you find a way to balance out your own emotions.

My Traumas

do this...not that

her: You want to be me. You copy everything I do!

YOU: Actually, you do inspire me. You're the exact type of mother, woman, wife and coparent I NEVER want to become.

her: (victim mode activated)

Ever been accused of being a copycat when that couldn't be further from the truth? While I DO NOT encourage you to respond to such outlandish accusations, I do want you to give credit where it's due. An adversary may actually represent the antithesis of your goals. When in doubt, look to them... and do the opposite!

Don't be bitter. Be better

I promise to be different from them because...

Over the course of my Stepfamily Coaching career, I began noticing a pattern in families and individuals that were caught in the toxic tango of conflict. I developed a system called AACEE. Accountability, acknowledgment, compassion, engagement, and empathy are the foundation of AACEE. This system requires people to carefully analyze their emotions before reacting. Over time and with a little practice, people began to experience mindset shifts, and they were challenged to assess their situation from a healthy perspective, which ultimately led them to more profound life experiences.

Give a detailed account of a conflict scenario you've recently faced. Discuss how it started, who was involved, and the conclusion of your conflict. Over the next few pages, use the definitions of the AACEE system and jot down how you can apply each word to your conflict. The goal is to figure out ways to either prevent it, redirect or change the outcome of the conflict.

Accountability

an obligation or willingness to accept responsibility or to account for one's actions

accountability
/əˌkaʊntəˈbɪlɪti/

Personal assessment

Acknowledgment

1. acceptance of the truth or existence of something

2. the action of expressing or displaying gratitude or appreciation for something

acknowledgement
/əkˈnɒlɪdʒm(ə)nt/

Personal assessment

Compassion

sympathetic pity and concern for the sufferings or misfortunes of others.

compassion
/kəmˈpaʃ(ə)n/

Personal assessment

Engagement

1. an arrangement to do something or go somewhere at a fixed time
2. a fight or battle between opposing forces

engagement
/ɪnˈɡeɪdʒm(ə)nt,ɛnˈɡeɪdʒm(ə)nt/

Personal assessment

Empathy

the ability to understand and
share the feelings of another

empathy
/ˈɛmpəθi/

Personal assessment

sometimes your brightest blessings show up wrapped in bullsh💩t

NajaHall.com

Don't let a crappy-looking circumstance deter you from getting to your blessings.
Remember, the trick of the enemy is to steal, kill, and destroy. Most hopes and dreams are squashed before they even have a chance to see the light of day because fear drowns them out.
Don't miss your blessing because you're distracted by someone that's already lost theirs.

I shall let no one steal my blessing

NAJA SAYS

A mother that deliberately restricts a relationship between a loving father and their child is an unhappy person.

She can be remarried, have a ton of new babies and profess to be the happiest clam in the dish, BUT if she is deliberately interfering with the relationship between her children and their father, she's STILL NOT HEALED.

An unhealed person can infest and affect your mind. Today you will evict them from taking up space in YOUR most valuable piece of real estate.

TRY THIS INSTEAD...

I'm sorry ~~if you feel~~ I've hurt you.

NAJA HALL

When we've hurt someone, it's important to acknowledge the pain we've caused. Giving a half-assed apology is the easiest way to show that you're out of touch with the pain you've caused and it lacks accountability. Next time, look them in the eye and humbly say, "I'm sorry." Don't offer any explanations, if's, and's or but's. Just allow them to simmer in the good flow of being acknowledged and allow them to speak.

THIS is how you apologize.

Reflections

naja says

It's not your responsibility to show people that are committed to mistreating that you're a good person.

Your responsibility is to NEVER become like them.

THE NASTY PEOPLE.

DON'T BE THEM.

THEY ARE THE ANTITHESIS OF HOW YOUR STORY SHOULD READ.

BE BETTER.

YOUR STEPKIDS ARE NOT
OBLIGATED TO LOVE YOU.
AND YOU'RE NOT OBLIGATED TO
LOVE THEM.
YOU ARE OBLIGATED TO LOVE
YOURSELF.

Reflections

RANDOM THOUGHTS

It's important to recognize that our loved one's decisions CAN affect our ability to be involved in their lives like we used to be. Sometimes you're required to STEP UP for them in their time of need. But other times, you'll have to STEP AWAY- when their life choices conflict with yours.

It doesn't mean they're bad, it just means you two need to learn to exist parallel for a while without intersectionality. Sometimes letting go gracefully can be the best way to build some type of new relationship with the person they're becoming.

Letting go is something some people master, and others can never quite seem to get it right. Sure, living a life of detachment keeps you safe, but you'll surely miss out on the genuine connections that make life colorful.

On the contrary, the need to be always attached leads to unhealthy dependency.

Finding that healthy medium is when you've hit the sweet spot. Being vulnerable enough to attach but being secure enough to let go is such a peaceful way to be.

Sucks when we have to let go of someone we care for because their choices disrupt our energy. Adulting is hard sometimes.

Reflections

Sis!
You can't care more than your man!

Pull up a chair and have a seat.

NAJA HALL. | @VIPSTEPMOM

Riddle me this? Why do you have your panties in a bunch while your man is sipping lemonade, as happy as a clam on a sunny day? So many stepmoms try to help their man fight the big bad monster and end up getting scars.

Today Stepsista, I need you to sit your cute a$$ down and focus on that which is in your control.

Your man realized he couldn't control his kid's mom a long time ago (which is why he's with you) so follow his lead! I swear he's not passive, gullible, or weak. He's just sick of the BS. In fact, I can guarantee he's tired of you talking about the drama all the time! It's consumed your life, your relationship, and your mind. STOP IT!

I'm so Bothered because...

BRITTLE NARCISSISM

The self-confidence of a narcissist is as brittle as an eggshell.

Narcissists don't move back and forth on a continuum of self-esteem as the rest of us do.

Under her fragile, brittle cover lies a hidden pool of insecurity and pain. Deep down, the narcissist's deepest and most powerful fear is that she is WORTHLESS.

Unless she has an innate desire to be different, she will never be able to like, nor accept you because she neither likes nor accepts herself. LET GO OF THE HOPE THAT YOU'LL BE ABLE TO COEXIST PEACEFULLY WITH THE NARCISSIST. The self-confidence of a narcissist is as brittle as an eggshell.

Narcissists don't move back and forth on a continuum of self-esteem as the rest of us do. Under her fragile, brittle cover lies a hidden pool of insecurity and pain. Deep down, the narcissist's deepest and most powerful fear is that she is WORTHLESS.

Thoughts

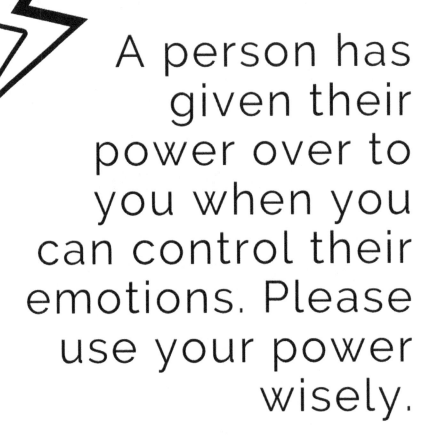

A person has given their power over to you when you can control their emotions. Please use your power wisely.

Are you dealing with someone whose panties always seem to be in a bunch at the mere mention of your name?

Girlfriend is bothered by you, so be a big girl and don't taunt her. Although she may deserve to be read her rights, hold your tongue and USE your power over her to speak LIFE.

Speak Life

you have I ever mistreated your kids?

her no

you did I break up your relationship w/ their dad?

her no

you so why do you act like this?

her I just don't like you

you 🏃 girl, f*ck you

Lemme get this straight? You're good to HER kids but she's committed to misunderstanding you. She wants to continue an invisible vendetta. She wants to stay in her feelings as opposed to finding a resolution.
Don't negotiate and convince anyone to see the good in you, RUN!

If someone is committed to disliking you, stay as far away from them as you can. Put away your olive branch and white flag. Resolve to surrounding yourself with people that LOVE you.

Reflections

Relationships are about relating. In both good and bad relationships, people agree/disagree on a common set of interests. In order for a bad relationship to transition into a good one, both sides must be equally invested in finding the most suitable solution for the matter at hand. The need to feel vindicated or "right" will almost always derail attempts at reconciliation. BOTH parties must acknowledge and accept the stance of the other person as it relates to the GREATER GOOD....and be willing to hug it out and commit to moving the F*CK on.

thoughts

How do you and your partner decompress after an episode of attack from a high conflict coparent?

It's so important to have a system in place when your energy is under attack. So often, nasty texts, conversations or emails from unhinged personality types can throw you off balance. What you must understand and accept is they do not have a healthy way of resolving conflict, and they are led by chaos. When they are in a manic episode, they aim to make sure everyone around them feels their pain, especially YOU.

USE YOUR FOOL AS YOUR FUEL!

Make love

Be still

Take a beat

Share an embrace

Choose your happiness

Don't let an enemy steal your joy

Form a habit of ignoring the drama

Be deliberate about staying focused

being a healthy stepmom means giving your heart away and accepting that you may not get it back

-Naja Hall

An excerpt from my journal:

I just dropped my husband and my stepkids off at the airport. He's taking them back to their other home today. We had a great summer and we've created so many memories. When we're all together, things are so seamless and easy. There is a calm that permeates our spirits and we feel peace. As a woman that has

weathered so many blended family storms, I value the 'normal ' moments so much.

Our summer has come to an end, but I feel so blessed to be graciously welcomed into the Hall family. In fact, after every visit, I thank the kids for being good, kind,

Pleasant, and welcoming me into the family with so much love. Also, instead of calling me Miss Naja, they started calling me MYNaja this summer. Not sure where that came from, but I like it.

PS, I pulled over and cried for a little while.

I feel joy because they are beautiful humans, but I feel pain because I must detach because I can only express love for them when they are with me. Being a healthy stepmom means giving your heart away and accepting that you may not get it back.

"The most common way people give up their power is by thinking they don't have any."
– Alice Walker

Don't believe the hype girlfriend. You are enough. You have power. Your opinion matters. Let your voice be heard and sing your song.

I've already won! Why am I still allowing myself to be dragged into a useless fight?

Wait, what have I won?

MY STEPKIDS' MOM IS
~~CRAZY!~~
INSECURE
FULL OF FEAR
DEVOID OF SELF WORTH
CODEPENDENT
CONSUMED WITH GUILT
ISOLATED
EMOTIONALLY UNINTELLIGENT
UNABLE TO BALANCE HER EMOTIONS
TRAUMATIZED

Frustration usually accompanies Co-Mothering with a biological mother who is less than ideal. Crazy is sort of a lazy way to describe the unhinged nature of moms that are unable (unwilling) to accept their child's stepmother. Her behavior is not a reflection of you. In fact, she is grateful that her kids are safe when they're with you. She is happy that they express love for you because she knows her kids could have an "evil stepmom'. She does not know how to thank or acknowledge you because chaos and conflict are what she is accustomed to. That's her safe space.

As opposed to letting her take you there, show compassion for her inner child... but steer clear of the Mean Woman that she is committed to being.

AT THIS VERY MOMENT, I FEEL...

secondhand embarrassment

personal embarrassment one feels for another who is making a fool of herself

We've all had our fair share of cringy stepmom moments, but one of the most common cases of secondhand embarrassment that happens is when a HCBM makes a pass at your man.

Check out this Member Submitted Post:

My husband and I have been dealing with a super high conflict mom for 7 years now. She's a special kind. Since she filed for divorce, she's had 5 boyfriends. We only know about all the different men because she sends my husband pictures of my stepkids with these guys, with the caption, "I've found your son a real dad. "I'm the only woman my husband has been with since their relationship ended btw. I'm sure everyone knows all the drama that comes along with this life, so there's no need to go into the dirty details of the depths of the craziness she's put our family through. Last year, after some coercing from her family, she began 'playing nice'. She did not interfere with visits, she 'allowed' him to openly communicate with the kids and she'd send him funnies about their children. Well, she's on man number 6, and she claims to be happy. Although she doesn't allow me to speak to the kids when they're with her, she nudges him to say hi when she calls the kids during our time.

Well, after she's raised hell all summer, my husband got his dad to return the kids to her home because we'd decided to take a mini-vacation. Apparently, she was expecting my man to drop the kids off because she had on a teeny shirt and some itty-bitty shorts. My father in law said she looked purely humiliated when she opened the door and saw that her baby daddy wasn't on the other side! Her face looked flushed and she got all sheepish. She didn't even greet her kids, who'd been away all summer! My FIL said, "It was a sorry sight to see. "I guess she was miffed because she has my husband blocked from contacting the kids.

Poor Thing

Today is going to be a good day because...

MAKE ME YOUR BENEFICIARY SO I KNOW IT'S REAL

THEY DIED, NOW WHAT?

Friendly reminder StepSistas, have you ensured that your man has removed ex's name from his work benefits, insurance benefits, etc.? Have you taken out policies on one another? If not, consider this a #LoveTapFromMissNaja. Handle your biz asap! Life is happening, and I've heard too many horror stories of death benefits going to an ex simply because no one thought to cross their t's and dot their I's.

NOTES...

If I was a teacher, these are a few of the courses I'd offer our children:

- How to handle rejection

- Dealing with a broken heart

- Identifying mental illness

- How to refuse sex

- Controlling your emotions

- The art of saying NO

- Accountability 101

- Emotional Intelligence

najahall.com

I'm just brainstorming, but it seems like we need to begin teaching our youth about calibrating their emotions before they become angry, imbalanced adults.

Reflections

naja says...

My favorite b-word is...

Ok ok... my second favorite B-word is BLOCK! BLOCK! BLOCK!
Please do not hesitate to exercise your right to block certain people from being able to call, text, email or send a raven to you! If there is a person in your life that can't seem to maintain a relationship with you based on BOUNDARIES and RESPECT, they gotta go!!! Today, I want you to cut ties with things and people that cost you your peace!

DEEP DOWN, I'M AFRAID THAT...

How do I show love to a child that is not allowed to like me?

Above all else, guard your heart, for everything you do flows from it.
Proverbs 4:23

You will never do anything right in the eyes of a jealous person

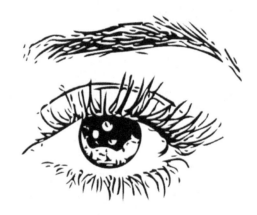

NAJA HALL

**Your time and energy are best spent on people that appreciate and understand your value.
As my Granddaddy used to say, "You're pissing in the wind" if you're hoping to gain acknowledgment and acceptance from a jealous person.**

Stepmom

Nutrition Facts

Serving Size: 1 Queen

Amount Per Serving

Calories: 0

% Daily Value

Boss Moves	100%
Brains & Beauty	100%
Perseverance	100%
Love	100%
Unbothered	100%
Class	100%
Pure Magic	100%
Finesse (drippin')	100%

Do you realize that you're a badass?! What are the 5 main ingredients that you throw in your queen sauce?

Stepkid: My mommy is getting married

SM: How nice!

Stepkid: Now I'll have 2  Dads!

SM:

This is usually how it goes in the blended family dynamic. Parents are generally their child's biggest influencer, so we get to shape the relationships our children form, and we groom them accordingly. Moms, when your child gains a stepmom, it's ideal to allow them to connect and honor them just as you would their stepdad. Dads, encourage your child to respect and accept their stepdad. When either parent holds their child in a loyalty bind (against a loving stepparent), it inhibits kids from relying on their own instinct when it comes to forming love bonds. The child becomes detached and conflicted and may misbehave. I know many adults that proclaim to hate their stepmoms yet view their stepdad as their Dad, and I cannot help but think how much influence their own mother may have had in hindering the bond.

If you're an alienated stepparent, keep your words few, never mention the parent that is causing strain, be kind, set firm boundaries and show your stepkid love, even when it seems impossible. If the child ultimately grows up to be self-aware and compassionate, they will recall that you were always good to them, and you can focus on developing a bond with them when they are no longer under the control of the parent that has placed an unfair obligation on them. They WILL see the light. You just have to remain in the light.

WOULD YOU MAINTAIN A RELATIONSHIP WITH YOUR STEPKIDS IF YOU BROKE UP WITH THEIR DAD?

What would happen if you ended your relationship with your stepchild's parent? Would you continue to be involved in their lives or would you just 'go away'?

Be honest

Some people will never accept you because you are a living, breathing reminder of their own failures.

NAJA HALL

The sooner you accept that 'they' cannot and will not accept you because of what YOU represent, the more peaceful your life becomes. Don't take it personally, it's really not you, it's them. Stop trying to force yourself in space where you're not welcome. If a person is unhealed, no amount of kindness and compassion will make them 'be nice' to you. Be okay with not being liked by 'them'! They barely even like themselves. 👀

PERSONAL REFLECTIONS

SOME PEOPLE
ARE HOLDING
GRUDGES
AGAINST YOU
FOR THE THINGS
THEY DID TO
YOU

Make it make sense

If you've spent years undermining your coparent's authority, you'll soon realize that the monster you created will EAT you too.

What goes around comes around. When you train a child to disrespect a loving parent or stepparent's authority, you are simultaneously teaching them that showing you respect is optional as well. Mark my words, you'll see.

A negative person will have a problem for every solution

Negative self-talk kills good vibes as long as something bad happens. Write down some recurring negative thoughts you face and then strikethrough them. Remember, we must be mindful of what we allow in our minds and out of our mouths because we have the power to manifest good and bad things in our lives.

Why do you resort to negative self-talk?

Very few humans are equipped to be wives, mothers, mental health gurus, paralegals, babysitters, romantic partners, and homemakers without cracking!
Somehow Stepmoms gets it DONE.

Many of my new Stepmom clients come to me in a panic because their man is distraught because of a high conflict coparent; their stepkids are unruly or because they are so lost in the madness that they're failing to focus on their most important job, being a Wife.

Reflections

Besides VIPStepmom (shameless plug, What are your favorite online stepmom communities?

Which friends and family members are your shoulders to lean on?

BRENDA SAYS

PRACTICE THE 5-5-5 RULE

If it's not going to matter in FIVE seconds FIVE minutes or FIVE months LET IT GO!

My friend, Brenda, who runs Stepmom Magazine talked about the 5-5-5 Rule on my podcast last week. She recollected all the time she wasted dealing with stuff that wasn't even important and she shared this ah-hah moment with us!!! Practicing the 5-5-5 rule is going to save you a lot of energy! I'm willing to bet a lot of the crap that's causing you to lose sleep, ain't even worth it.

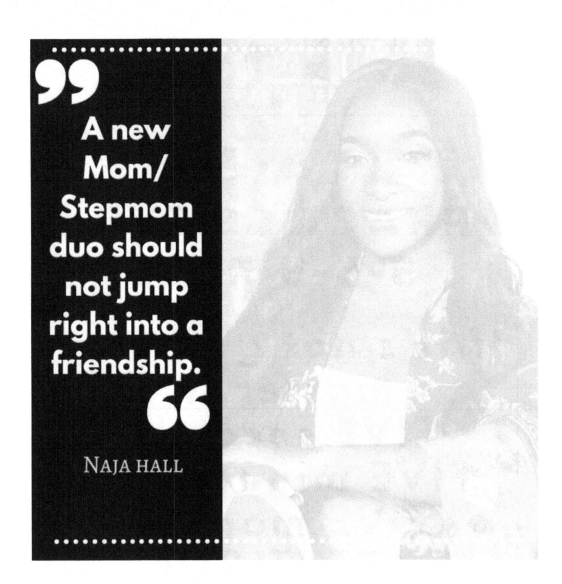

> A new Mom/ Stepmom duo should not jump right into a friendship.

NAJA HALL

We hear so many horror stories about the instant clash between Mothers and Stepmothers. If you're blessed enough to have a pleasant Mom in your life, I know you're tempted to dive head-first into a friendship with her! You're thinking, we could be "different." We could get matching t-shirts for the kids' soccer games. Heck, we could even go get our nails done together!

I'd advise you to be kind to her. But keep a respectful distance in the beginning. Take some time to understand how she defines friendship because with friendship comes responsibility and certain expectations.

Do offer a secondary line of communication but make it known that you are unable to be an intermediary. And do not expect the Mom to consider you in all dealings with the father of her children.

Should a friendship naturally develop, awesome, but the key priority is to ensure that your actions represent compassion to the children and tons of grace for yourself.

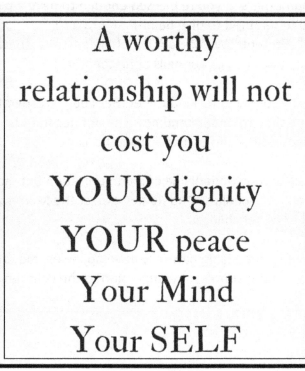

A worthy
relationship will not
cost you
YOUR dignity
YOUR peace
Your Mind
Your SELF

NAJA HALL
vipstepmom

No matter your race or religion, the patriarchal nature of our society expects and requires women to sacrifice themselves for their men and their families. Ladies, pick partners that recognize the disparity and that will do everything in their power to uplift YOU. I ain't sacrificing shit for a joker that hasn't made sure MY cup runneth over. Balance is key.

I FEEL MOST BALANCED WHEN

OVERWHELMED?

FULL OF ANXIETY?

ABOUT TO GIVE UP?

Are you seriously gonna let them run you away?

Reflections

Naja Hall ✔
@VIPStepmom

It is hard to show compassion to an individual who has no desire to extend compassion to you.
It is not impossible though.

Compassion is defined as a concern for the sufferings or misfortunes of others. Occasionally, we may come across an individual that intends to do us harm and they've made it known that they cannot show compassion on a basic human level. My advice for you is to remove yourself from this individual's grasp. If you must deal with such a person, guard ALL that is precious to you, mainly your peace of mind. Understand that this person sees herself as undeserving of love; therefore, they only know how to kill, steal, and destroy the love within others. By recognizing that which they lack, you are showing compassion.

Today I feel

If you are always in constant
conflict with someone, this may
be a sign that <u>one</u> of you may be
suffering from an undiagnosed
mental illness or personality
disorder. If you find yourself
walking on eggshells during
every interaction, you're
probably the sane one.

Constant conflict is not normal, nor is it healthy. If you're in a situation where you're always under attack, you do not have to accept this as the way it has to be. If you are the one inflicting the harm, seek help. If you're the person constantly getting dumped on, you especially need to seek help.

A *licensed therapist is qualified to diagnose mental illness and personality disorders.
A *psychiatrist can prescribe medications to treat mental ailments.
A *life coach helps you to achieve your personal goals and push through major life obstacles.

BORDERLINE

NARCISSISTIC

BIPOLAR

PARANOID

PSYCHO

SCHIZO

ANTI SOCIAL

OBSESSIVE

DISASSOCIATIVE

ANXIOUS

HISTRIONIC

Personality disorders are classified by the American Psychiatric Association's *Diagnostic and Statistical Manual of Mental Disorders* (DSM) as mental illnesses. A **personality disorder** is a type of mental **disorder** in which you have a rigid and unhealthy pattern of thinking, functioning, and behaving. A person with a **personality disorder** has trouble perceiving and relating to situations and people. Do your own research and jot down notes on traits that you've experienced within yourself and others.

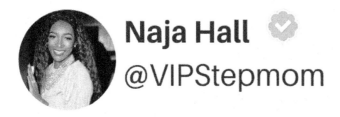

Naja Hall ✓

@VIPStepmom

You will continue to suffer if you have an emotional reaction to everything that is said to you. True power is sitting back and observing things with logic. If words control you, that means everyone else can control you. Breathe and allow things to pass.

Let's take control of our own emotions and not let our emotions control us!

Today I will focus on

How has being a stepmom decreased _or_ increased your quality of life?

I've been challenged to grow...

building a relationship with a sh*tty person is like baking a cake with rotten eggs

It's gonna stink, it will leave a bad taste in your mouth, it'll make you sick. I wish we all were as skilled at recognizing shitty people as we are rotten eggs.

Today's Reflections

It's a very sad and unnatural phenomenon to have to detach from your spouse's kids in between visits.
It's a very delicate balance.

All you can do is treat them kindly and hope that you can form a less constricted bond with them as they get older.

NAJA HALL

Stepparenting is hard because it goes against the natural order of things. In the wild, when a baby cub is raised by another mother, it's usually because the cub's biological mother is gone. In our lives, recoupling and remarriage force us to form bonds with children we did not bear. If we are blessed, a love bond develops.

The difficulty lies in the fact that the child is groomed by two different households; therefore, influence and time are limited as a stepparent. In tough cases, conflict between parents can hinder and isolate a stepparent. Being unable to show consistent love to a child that you care for because of silly-head grownups getting in the way isn't fair!

Chin up buttercup, your stepkids will grow up. For now, fill their minds with beautiful experiences. Overwhelm them with positive vibes and love. Support your Spouse, and if the children become good people, they will be open and free to love you back. Don't give up; the kids are just as anxious to love you as you are, them.

Today my personal mantra is

Stepmom Affirmations

I am worthy of love

I deserve a life of abundance

My presence provides a light in the lives of others

I will give love away every chance I get

I know that love always drowns out hatred

I am bigger, faster and stronger than others think

I will no longer cower to protect the feelings of people that treat me badly

I will set firm boundaries when I am disrespected

I will only consider the opinions of people that are invested in my growth

I love myself

I am happy with my life

I can do anything

I am good

I am whole

I am loved and valued

Write down some Affirmations of your own

In general

Kids are assholes

My kids

Your kids

Their kids

All kids

It's tough NOT to take things personally when we feel stepkids are being disrespectful because we don't know their motives. Do you know what their motives are??? Kids are jerks! When you find yourself feeling triggered, take a beat and give the kid the benefit of the doubt. Jot down a moment when you felt crossed by a stepchild. How could you have redirected your feelings to a place of compassion?

STEPKIDS WITH HCBMS AND ABSENT BMS ARE TOUGHER TO LOVE.

It can feel impossible to connect with your stepchild because they have a mother that makes your Stepmom experience harder. Be mindful that stepkids grow up, and they could possibly see that their mother was not right. They will remember how you made them feel. Embrace them if they show you that they need affection. Give them an open invitation to love you. No matter what, make sure they can never say that you were unfair to them. Have you found yourself detaching from your stepkids because of their mother?

TELL YOUR MAN

no.

IS A COMPLETE SENTENCE

Although you try to be a tough guy, those rare moments when your stepkids show you love and affection make your heart melt. It's okay to allow yourself to have hope.

I feel most hopeful when...

Instead of thinking about the bullshit that I can't control, I could be...

and...

Things I love about my relationship...

Share these positive affirmations with your man...

ASSIGNMENT FOR HIM

Ask your man to answer a few questions for you. You will refer to this page during the tough times.

I FELL FOR YOU BECAUSE

I FEEL MOST IN LOVE WITH YOU WHEN

I WILL ALWAYS CHOOSE YOU BECAUSE

YOU MAKE MY LIFE BETTER BECAUSE

I WOULD LIKE MORE

I'D APPRECIATE LESS

WHEN I SEE YOU HURTING, I FEEL

I WISH YOU KNEW

If it doesn't affect

You

or

Your household

It ain't **YOUR** concern

I hope you dance.....

Music has a way of taking our minds to nostalgic places. A great song allows us to reminisce and simply feel good. Think of 11 songs that make your heart smile. Jot these down and make yourself a Stepmom playlist. Whenever you feel low, press play!

Sometimes, Ignorance can be bliss.

Ask Naja

BM just called my Husband and told him that my stepkids said I am lazy and boring. She has always been so negative and she is bothered by the fact that my stepkids really like me. She has been more intentional about being mean since we had an *ours baby*.

Naja Says

I'd advise you to tell hubby to STRICTLY share things that affect **your** money, **your** marriage and **your** household. It's his job to filter out the bullshit. This is bullshit.

And frankly, it's none of your business what a nonfactor thinks of you. She is a nonfactor.

From a parenting perspective, advise your man to gently speak to the children because their words may have been twisted or completely falsified. Kids with rude moms should be made aware that anything they share about their other household may be turned into something negative and divisive. It is your husband's job to use these teachable moments to instill basic human decency, discretion, and compassion in his children.

Finally, this is ALL his mess. Stay focused on what matters most. Our men have to learn to put out fires without dragging us into it. In this case, ignorance is bliss.

TODAY'S MANTRA

I refuse to be a repository for negative people and negative thoughts.

Make a list of things that you wish your partner NEVER shared with you. Discuss how they have affected you. Lastly, what have you done to purge these things from your space?

Basic Rule of Stepmomming

Be flexible

 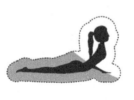 

We bend BUT we don't break

pro tip

treat your stepkids like you're a cool ass Auntie

We are influenced by many different people. Think about women, aside from your biological mother that have made a positive impact on your life. Discuss what they did or said to make you feel special and acknowledged. Take these small nuggets and repeat the actions or sentiments with your stepkids.

When your stepkids
refer to your "ours baby"
as their half-brother,
Ask them, which half
they will love?

YOUR BIOLOGICAL & STEP CHILDREN MAY FEEL JEALOUS OF YOUR NEW BABY. HOW WILL YOU PREPARE THE OLDER CHLDREN TO RECEIVE THEIR NEW SIBLING?

you have not been condemned to live your life at a reduced capacity because you've fallen for a man with kids

Sometimes it feels like Stepmotherhood is a sentence you've been stuck with. Use this page to complain about how much it sucks.

Today, I will be intentional about manifesting positivity into my life. I will protect my heart. I will purge all bad thoughts. I will constantly reaffirm myself. I was born to thrive, not just survive. I only have ONE life to live and I will not spend another day feeling sorry for myself or lamenting over my circumstances.

I WILL THRIVE BECAUSE...

Check out the 1ˢᵗ book in the Girl, Bye! series.

Visit www.GirlBye.info

In *Girl, Bye! She's Not Going Anywhere…Neither Are You*, author Naja Hall sends a loud and clear message to Mothers and Stepmothers stuck in the throes of conflict. While it would be nice for Moms and Stepmoms to become great friends, that is usually a far-fetched reality for most. Neither of these women are excited about the other's presence, so this pairing is likely to be met with apprehension, confusion, and plenty of headaches. While *she* may not be ready to leave the drama at the door, *YOU* don't have to answer every time trouble comes knocking.

Naja compels women to be the highest version of themselves despite the presence of a woman that contradicts her expectations and challenges her peace. Naja also teaches tactics on silencing the lingering doubts and fears that plague the minds of these women. Not one to stray from her roots as Stepfamily Coach, Naja compels women to explore the Mother or Stepmother in their lives. They will also confront their own idiosyncrasies and figure out why *the other woman's* presence bothers them so much.

Girl, Bye! has been declared better than **"six months of therapy in a paperback book!"**

*As an addition, Naja walks you through each chapter in the Daily Video Lessons. The videos, eBook and paperback book are available at www.GirlBye.info

Join my private Stepmom community

VIPSTEPMOM.COM

For less than a glass of wine, you get:

VIP access to video interviews

You will have full access to candid monthly chats with my guru pals. This video series will dig deep into stepmothering as it relates to love, marriage, mental health, and a wide array of issues that affect women like us. Not to be a name dropper, but I know some pretty influential subject matter experts and they will be dedicating years of experience to our community.

Good stuff straight to your inbox

Throughout the month, I will be sending downloadables, videos, podcasts, eBooks and written content to you. Aside from our members-only content, VIP Stepmoms will have access to my database of curated picks from around the web. No need to scour the internet when you need help. VIPStepmom is your hub for all-things-stepmom related!

VIP Stepmom podcast

Stepmoms need a little extra love, so each month I'll be hosting the VIPStepmom podcast. It is juicy, unfiltered and all about YOU. This podcast is for US, by US so members of our community will be the driving force behind each episode.

Anonymous Discussion Forum

Our discussion forum is totally anonymous and it is strictly available to community members. Each month, I will peruse the forum for the top questions and comments and address them in a Q&A video session.

Class is in Session!

A Rose and Blxx membership gets you lifetime access my new courses, classes and worksheets.

Monthly StepMom Magazine

StepMom Magazine is the longest running professional journal for women in families like ours. I've partnered with them to deliver monthly issues straight to your inbox! VIP Members not only get access to current issues of StepMom magazine, but I've loaded tons of back issues in our database.

Group Coaching

Group Coaching sessions are interactive, live events hosted by me or an expert that I've invited. They typically take place at the end of the month, but I'll always email you a heads-up so you don't miss the fun! Members are encouraged to participate! Join a video call or observe incognito- without fear of judgment.

Discounts on Private Coaching

Members get discounted private coaching with me and my group of coaches. You also have access to the appointment calendar so you call (or Facetime) when you're in need of solution-based power hour. Think of a laser session as the mashup of a motivational speech and pouring your heart out to a best friend…that happens to be an expert.

ABOUT THE AUTHOR

NAJA HALL is a Master Stepfamily Coach and the founder of the largest online communities for millennials in stepfamilies, Blended and Black & VIPStepmom. Naja hosts a top-ranked podcast called *I Know I'm CRAZY.* She also contributes written and video content for numerous national media outlets. She resides in New York City with her husband, and she is a stepmom of 3.

Websites: NajaHall.com, GirlBye.info, BlendedandBlack.com, and VIPStepmom.com

Connect on Instagram, Facebook, Twitter, Pinterest, and YouTube

@BlendedandBlack @VIPStepmom

Made in the USA
Coppell, TX
14 February 2020